BERKLEE PRESS

Improvisation *for* FLUTE

The Scale/Mode Approach

ANDY McGHEE

Berklee Press

Vice President: David Kusek
Dean of Continuing Education: Debbie Cavalier
Chief Operating Officer: Robert F. Green
Managing Editor: Jonathan Feist
Editorial Assistants: Yousun Choi, Emily Goldstein, Claudia Obser
Cover Designer: Kathy Kikkert

ISBN 978-1-4234-6740-3

1140 Boylston Street
Boston, MA 02215-3693 USA
(617) 747-2146

Visit Berklee Press Online at
www.berkleepress.com

DISTRIBUTED BY

HAL•LEONARD®
CORPORATION
7777 W. BLUEMOUND RD. P.O. BOX 13819
MILWAUKEE, WISCONSIN 53213

Visit Hal Leonard Online at
www.halleonard.com

Dedicated to my wife Connye and my brother
Tom whose faith in me made this possible.

Andy McGhee

CONTENTS

PREFACE

Since joining the faculty of Berklee College of Music in 1966, I have instructed hundreds of students in jazz improvisation. Not only saxophonists, but trumpet, violin, and flute playing pupils were interested in learning or improving their skills at improvisation.

My first statement to each of them and to you is that there are no shortcuts in learning to improvise well. You must develop your ear to hear what you want to play and perfect your techniques so that you can play what you hear. The next important tip I give to my students is to listen to good players and imitate. Some students initially resent that they are advised to imitate or as it were, copy, until it is explained that this not only develops the ear and technique, but also gives the student an understanding or feeling as to what can be played and how a certain sound is achieved.

This book is simply an organized presentation of what is being played and a step-by-step guide to the development of *your* improvising skills.

As I will remind you throughout the book, the very best way to apply what you are learning is to get together with a rhythm section, or at least a piano or guitar player, after you get the notes of the various exercises and phrases under your fingers. By hearing the chord or tonality while you are playing the associated notes, you will naturally develop your sense of listening and hearing.

Listening, practice, and experience all work together to develop the skills necessary for you to do your own jazz improvising.

Andy McGhee

AUTHOR'S NOTES

The modes and scales used in this book are presented in such a way as to answer and simplify the many questions about modal playing and improvisation. Please note that only the most commonly used and useful modal scales are presented.

To simplify the seven modes, the following chart outlines the mode and the chord with which it is most often associated in improvisation. Notice that the Ionian mode is actually a major scale. Being able to play with ease the major scale in all keys will simplify playing in all the other modes.

Mode Name	Degree of Major Scale	Chord Symbol usually associated	Chord name and Chord in Key of C
Ionian	(Major Scale)	I maj7 or I6	C maj7 (C6)
Dorian	(2nd degree)	II-7	D-7
Phrygian	(3rd degree)	III-7	E-7
Lydian	(4th degree)	IV maj7	F maj7
Mixolydian	(5th degree)	V7	G7
Aeolian (Natural Minor)	(6th degree)	VI-7	A-7
Locrian	(7th degree)	VII-7(♭5)	B-7(♭5) or B♯7

The Modes presented in this book may be applied to your playing and improvisation in two basic ways.

The first way is to apply the Modal scales and exercises to Modal tunes or sections of tunes. These are the 'pure' unaltered Modes and are often seen in modern music in lieu of conventional 'chord changes', as in the following example.

F Lydian   **A Dorian**

The second way is to use the various modal scales as guides to the notes that can be played when improvising on chord changes. In this case, as illustrated in the next example, the Modal scale used would depend upon the type [function] of chord change indicated in the tune.

D-7 (use D Dorian)   **G7 (use G Mixolydian)**

You will notice in using this book that by making a simple alteration in certain modes (by raising or lowering particular notes) new scales are produced which give you the notes available for nearly every type of chord change. The following examples show you two such alterations included in this book and basically how they are used.

Lydian Mode   used with   **F maj7**   **Lydian** *Flat 7* **Scale**   used with ♭**II7**
                              IV maj7   (and other chords)

Chapter I

The Dorian Mode

Though the Ionian Mode (major scale) is commonly used (in conjunction with the I chord) when playing on chord progressions, the Dorian mode is the most commonly used in "modal" playing. It is a scale beginning and ending on the 2nd degree of the major scale. "D" Dorian would be like a "C" major scale beginning and ending on "D."

The Dorian mode is most commonly applied in improvisation as the scale relating directly to the II-7 chord.

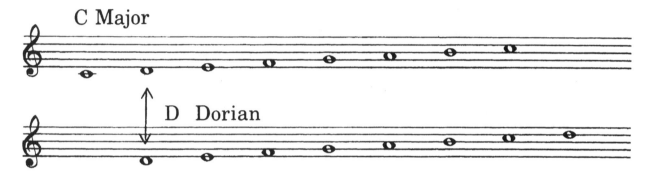

The II chord in a major key occurs naturally as a minor seventh chord. In the key of C, the II chord would be D-7.

1

scale   triads built on each degree of the scale

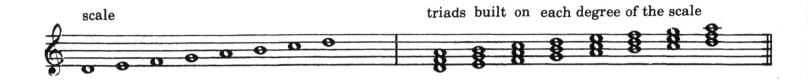

Exercises

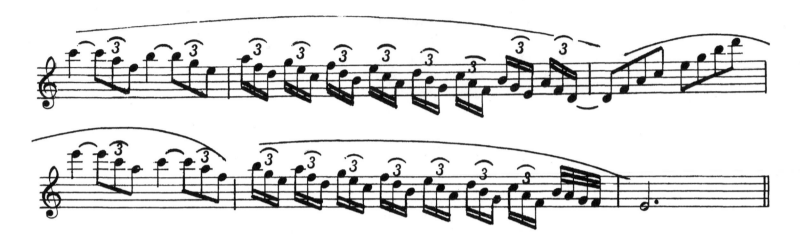

Sample four bar phrases in D Dorian.

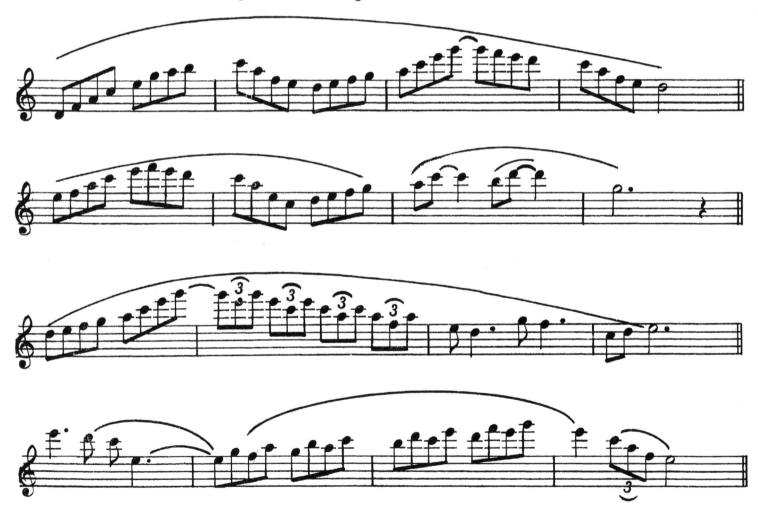

A Dorian

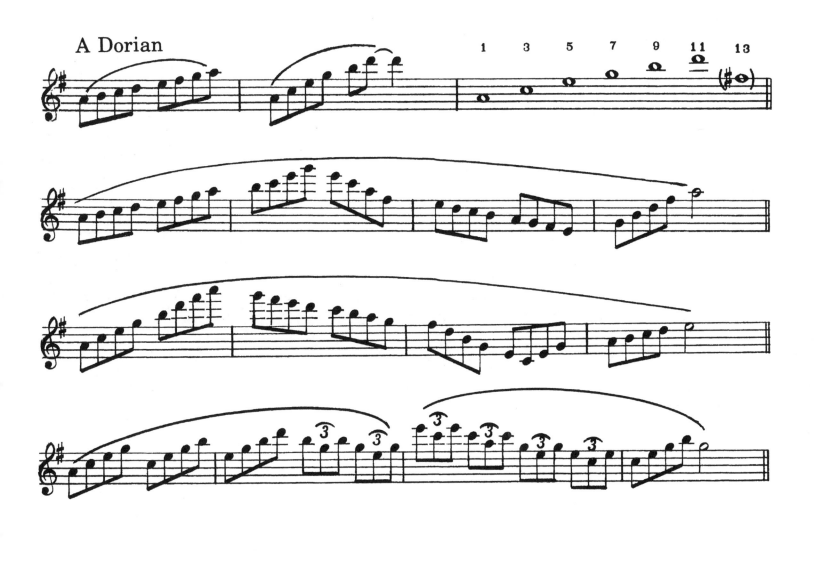

scale

triads built on each degree of the scale

Exercises

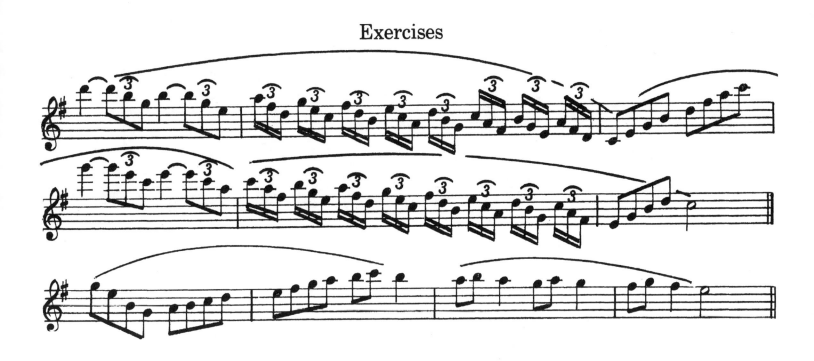

G Dorian

scale

triads built on each degree of the scale

Exercises

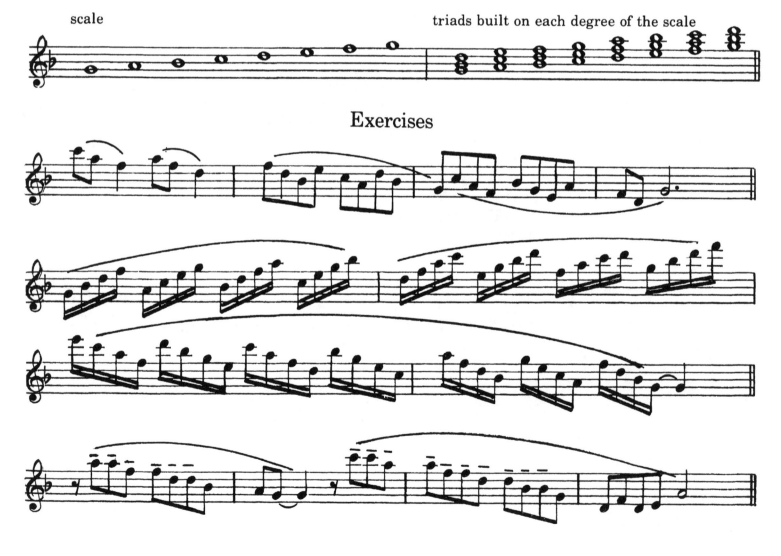

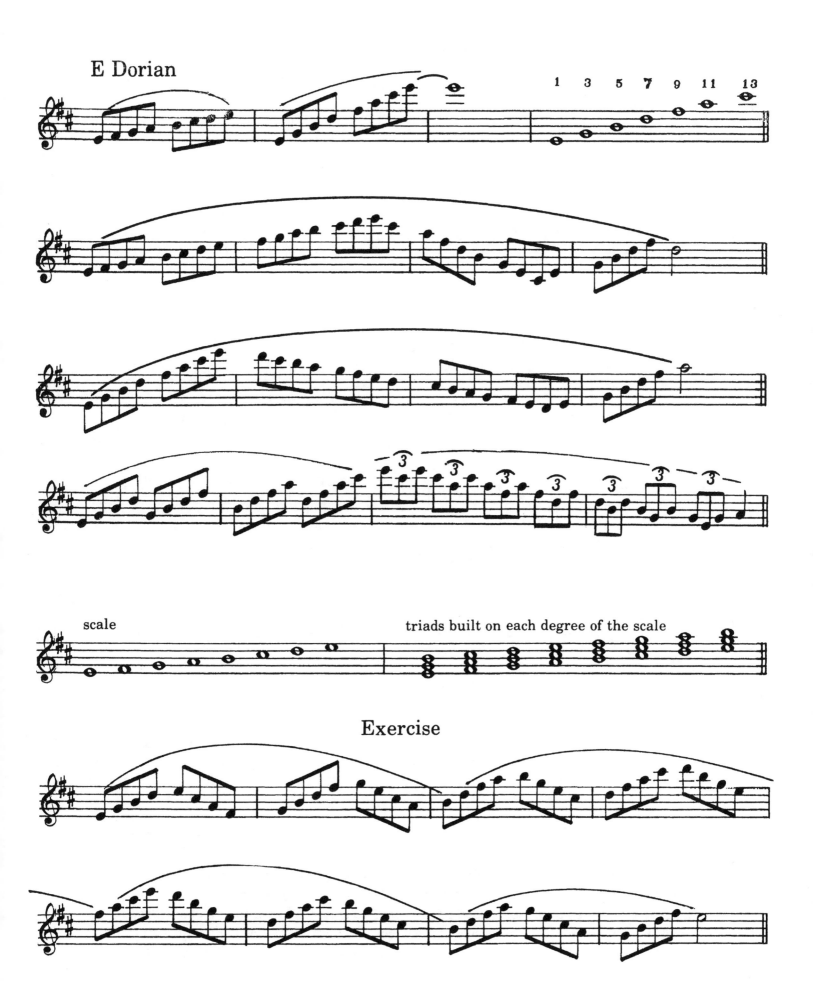

E Dorian

scale

triads built on each degree of the scale

Exercise

C Dorian

scale

triads built on each degree of the scale

Exercise

B Dorian

scale

triads built on each degree of the scale

Exercise

7

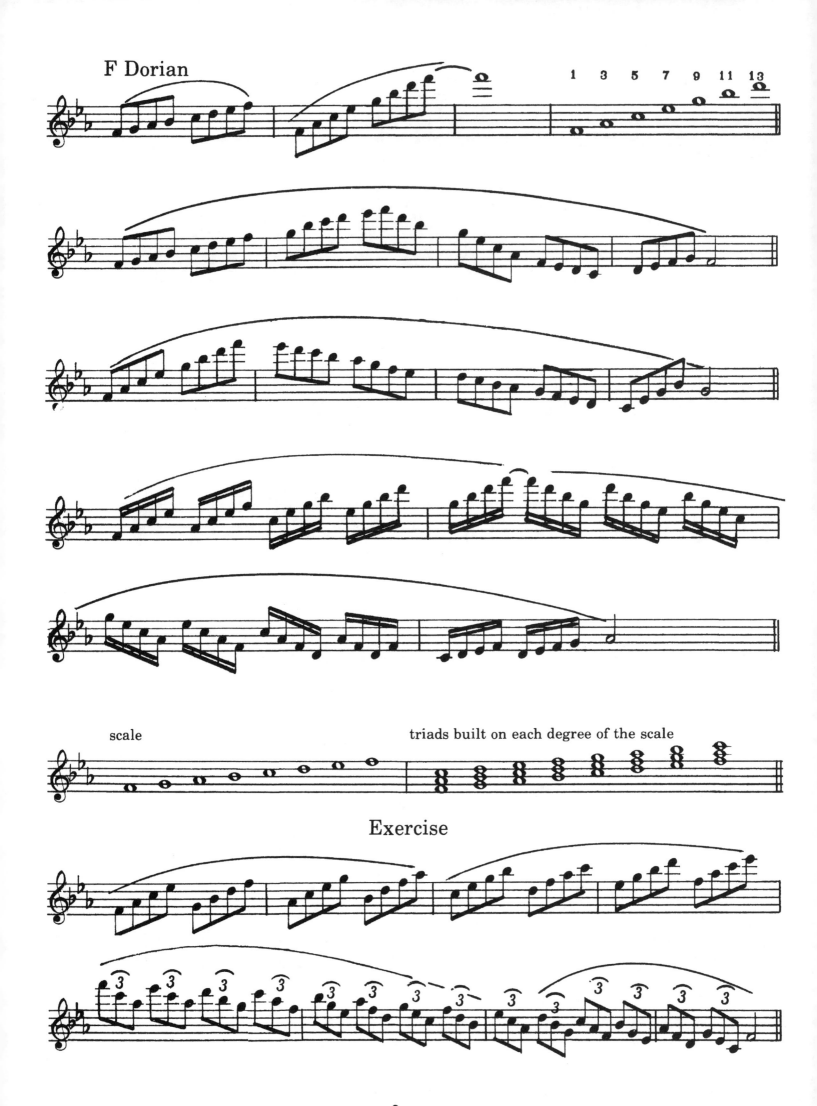

F Dorian

scale

triads built on each degree of the scale

Exercise

8

scale

triads built on each degree of the scale

Exercise

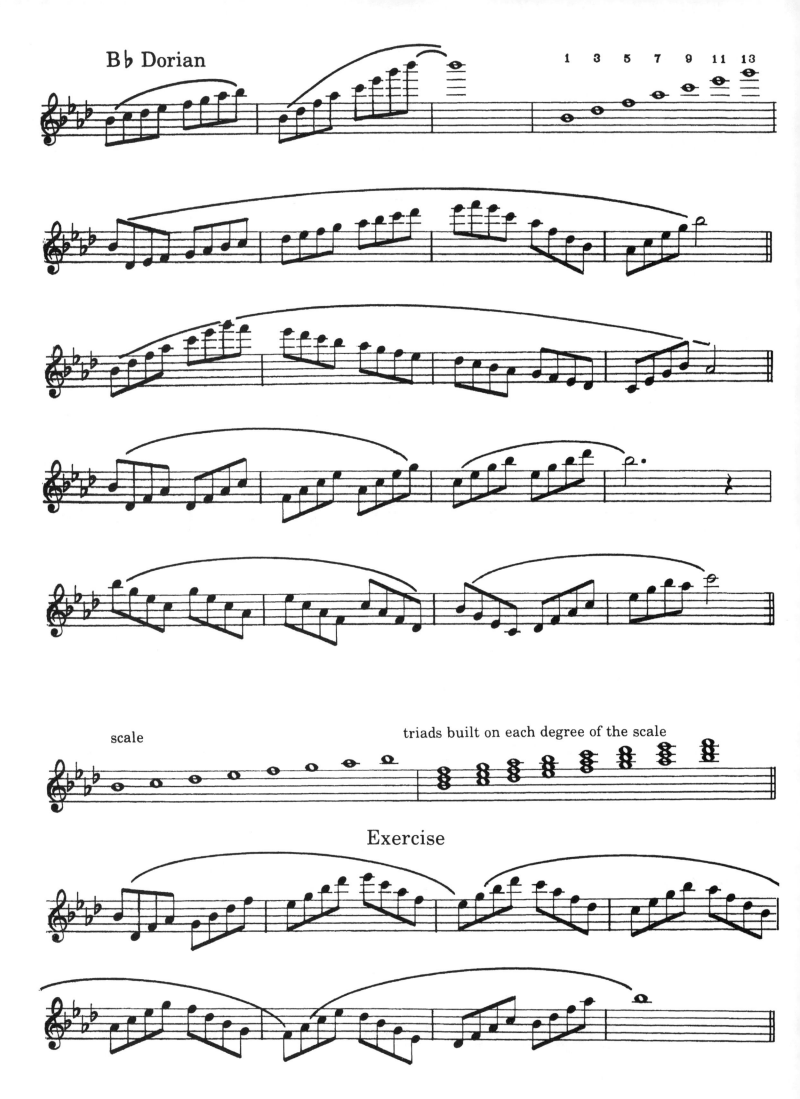

Bb Dorian

scale

triads built on each degree of the scale

Exercise

C# Dorian

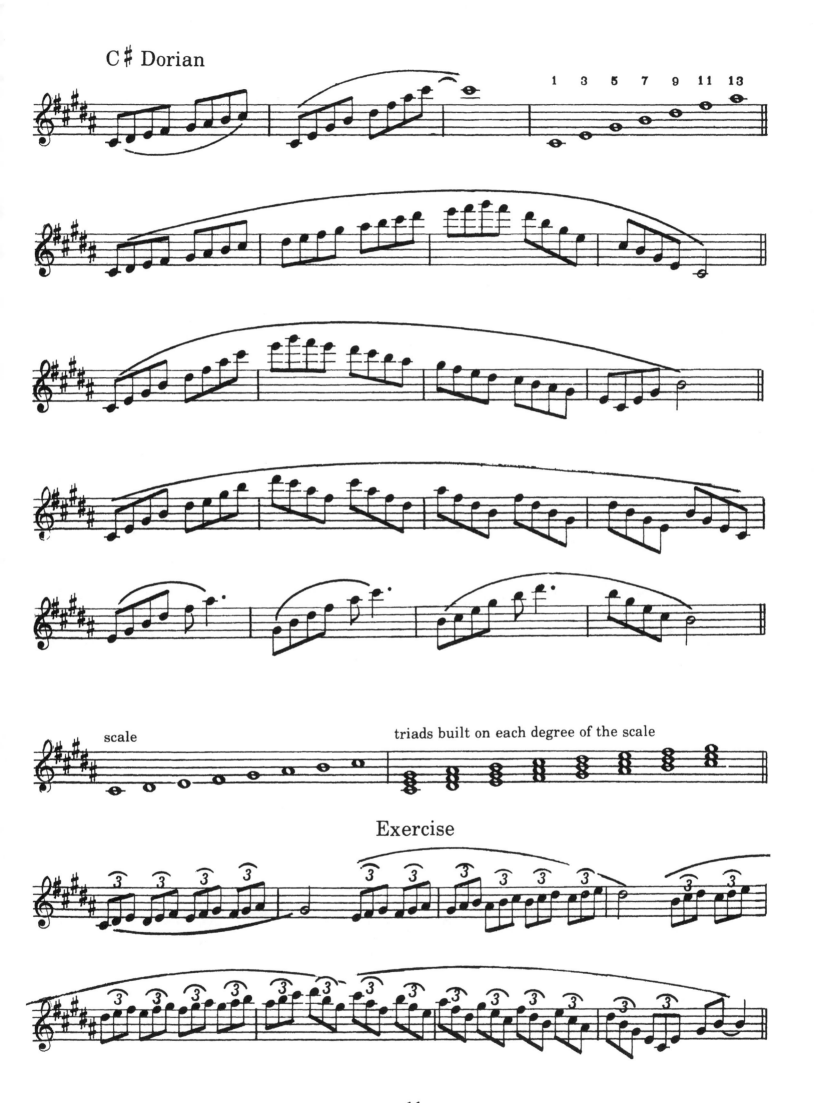

scale

triads built on each degree of the scale

Exercise

11

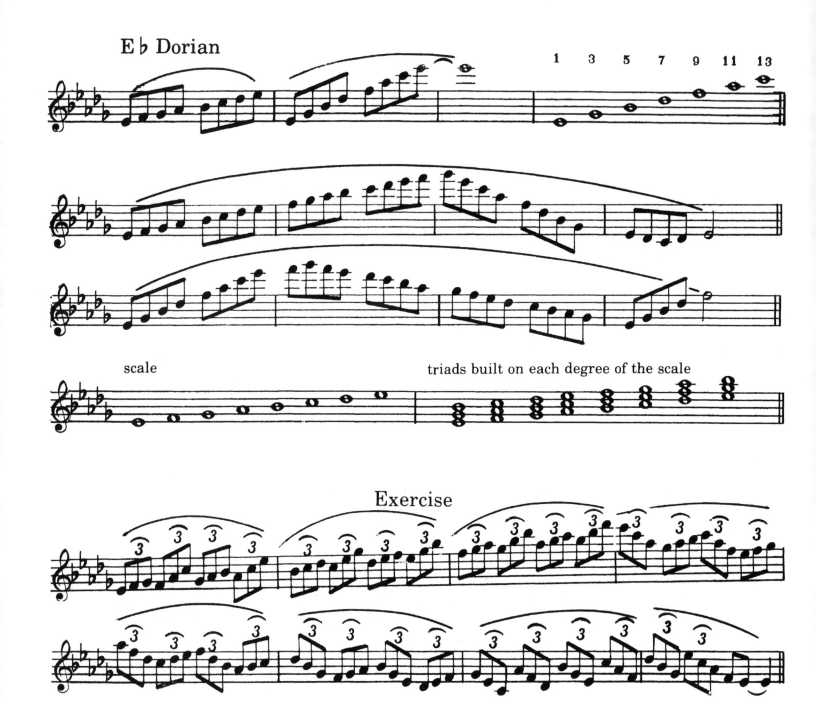

scale

triads built on each degree of the scale

Exercise

Play the following Mode scales and arpeggios. Begin very slowly to develop control and accuracy, then speed.

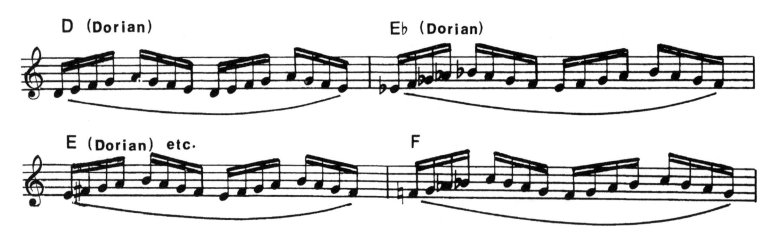

D (Dorian)

Eb (Dorian)

E (Dorian) etc.

F

13

Chapter II

The Mixolydian Mode

The Mixolydian mode is a scale beginning and ending on the fifth degree of the major scale. "G" Mixolydian would be like a "C" scale beginning and ending on "G." The Mixolydian mode is most commonly used in improvisation as the scale relating directly to the V7 chord.

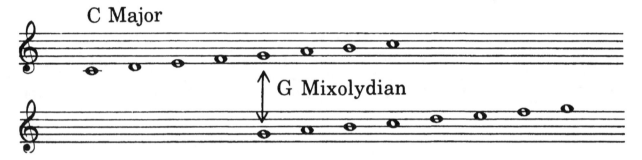

The V chord occurs naturally as dominant seventh. In the key of C, the V7 chord would be G7.

NOTE: *In this example the 11th is in parenthesis (). This is used throughout the book to indicate that this particular step of the scale (in this case the 11th) may be used as a passing tone while playing, but should generally be avoided for use as a prominent or emphasized tone.*

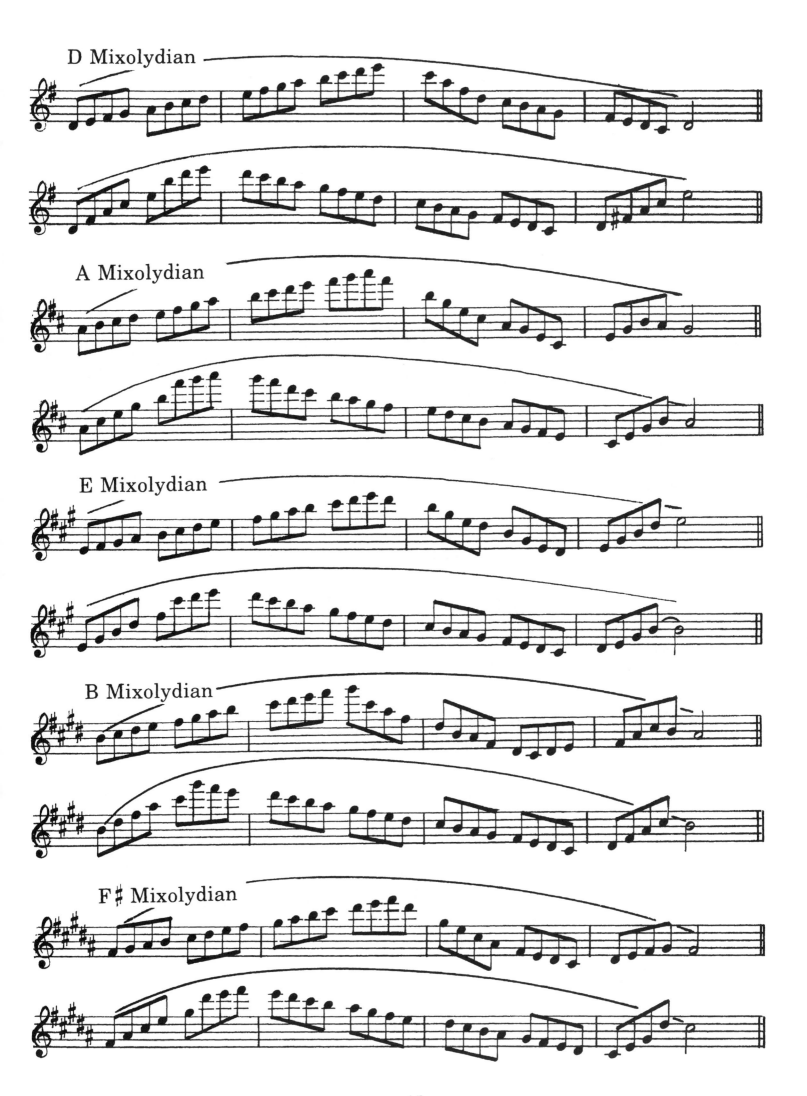

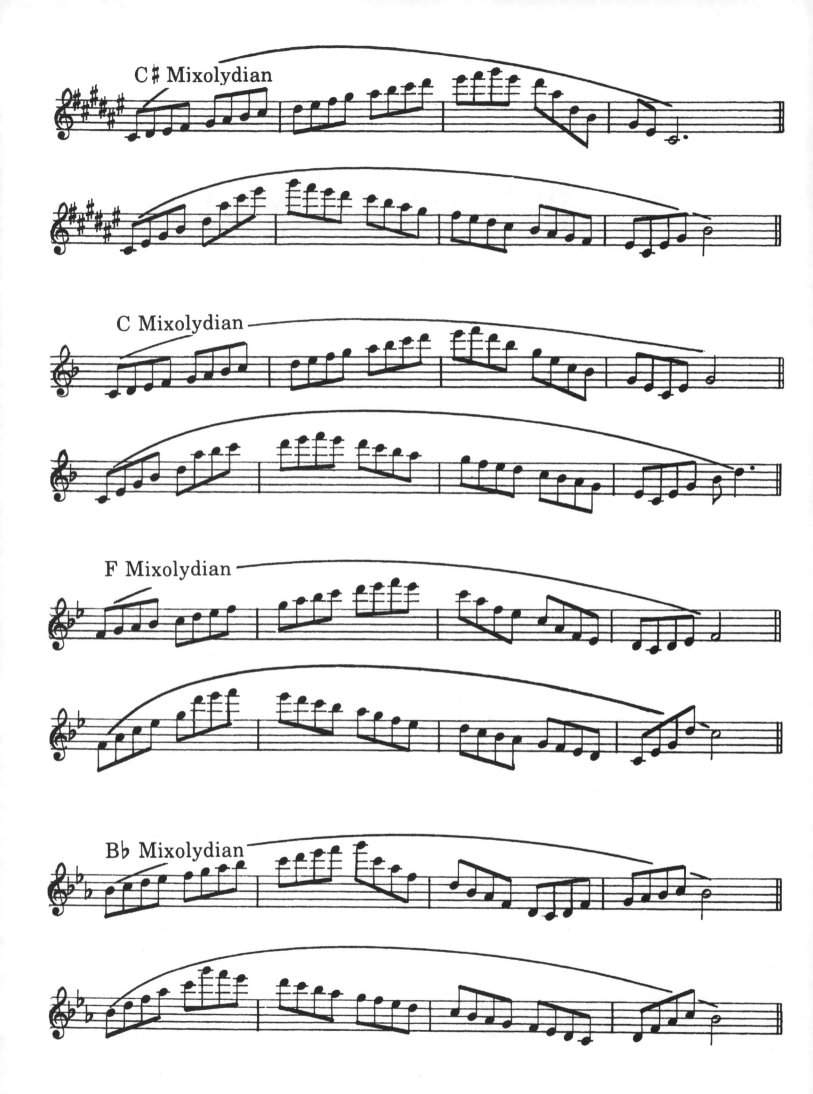

C♯ Mixolydian

C Mixolydian

F Mixolydian

B♭ Mixolydian

Here is the cycle of 5ths in the Mixolydian Mode through all of the keys.

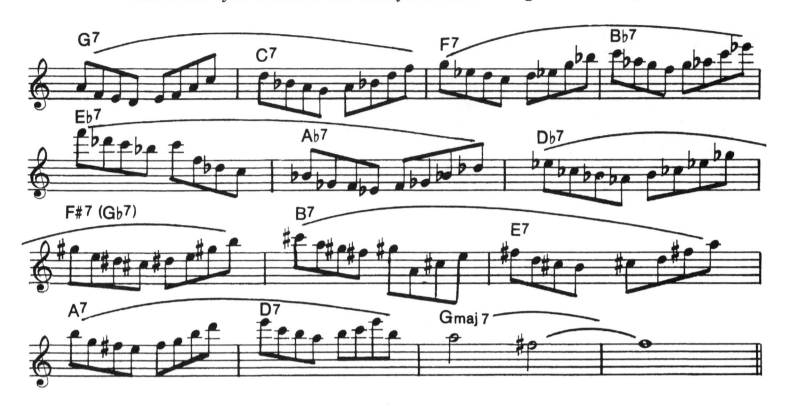

Here are some shorter patterns in the Mixolydian Mode.

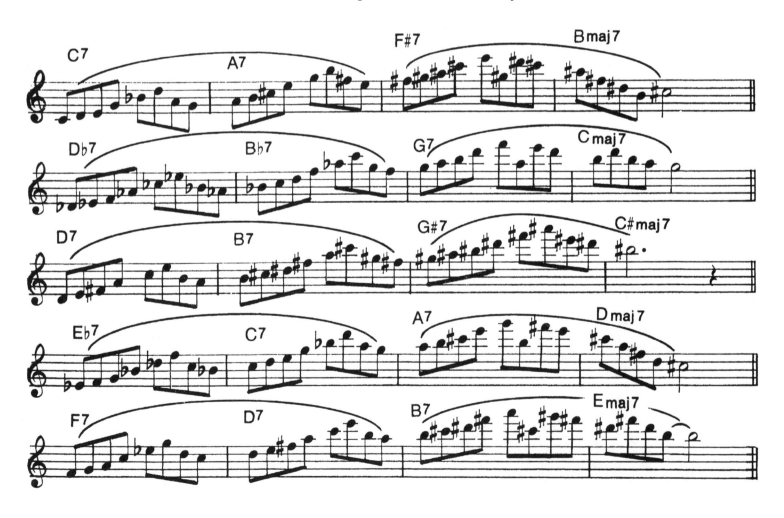

Eight bar patterns in the Mixolydian Mode.

The following four bar phrases are in sets of three. The first two in each set should be played as written. The third of each set, having only the first measure complete, should be finished in the same manner as the first two but in the indicated key. When you find that you can do this with ease, try each set of phrases by ear in all keys.

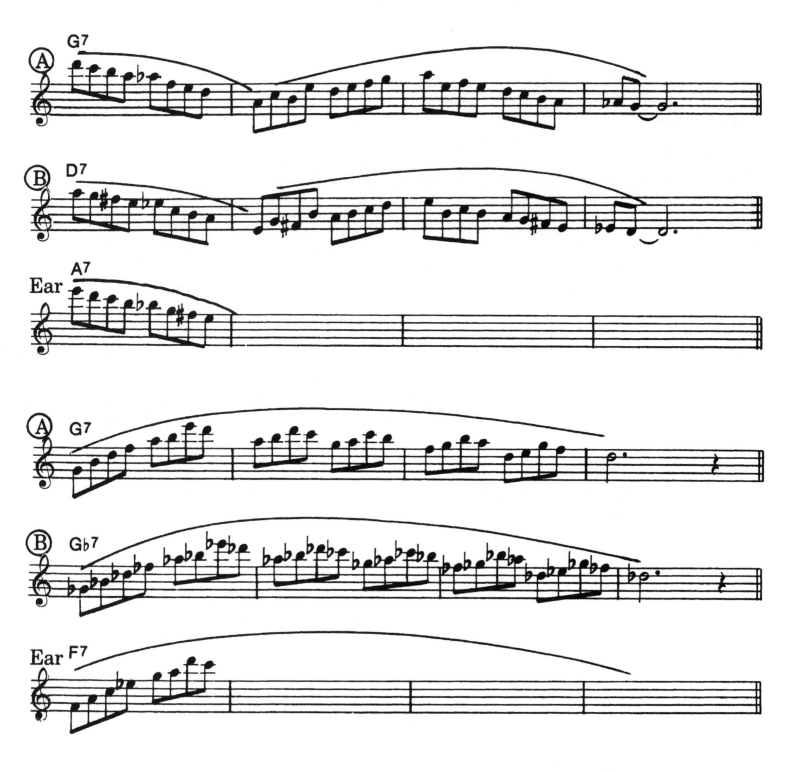

The following exercises should be played slowly, for control, and played with full tones.

Chapter III

Combining the Dorian
and Mixolydian Modes

II-7 to V7 Chord Progression

This chapter combines the Dorian (II-7) from Chapter I and the Mixolydian (V 7) from Chapter 2, to form the common chord progression, II-7 to V7. This progression is also known as sub-dominant to dominant and is used in nearly every tune written. You will notice that throughout this book, as new scales are introduced, they are put into chord progressions so that you will have a practical application of what you have learned. Including these scales into chord progressions also enables you to develop your ear to "hear" what to play in these progressions. To get the most benefit from these exercises, have a piano player or guitarist accompany you using the chord changes given above the notes.

NOTE: *The chord changes are written in the key of the instrument playing the exercise so that the accompanist must transpose (except for "C" instruments) to make them sound right.*

22

The following II-7 to V7 phrases also include the I maj7 chord so that you can feel and hear how these chord changes fit into a certain tonality. After each two bar phrase, you should get a feeling of finality or ending.

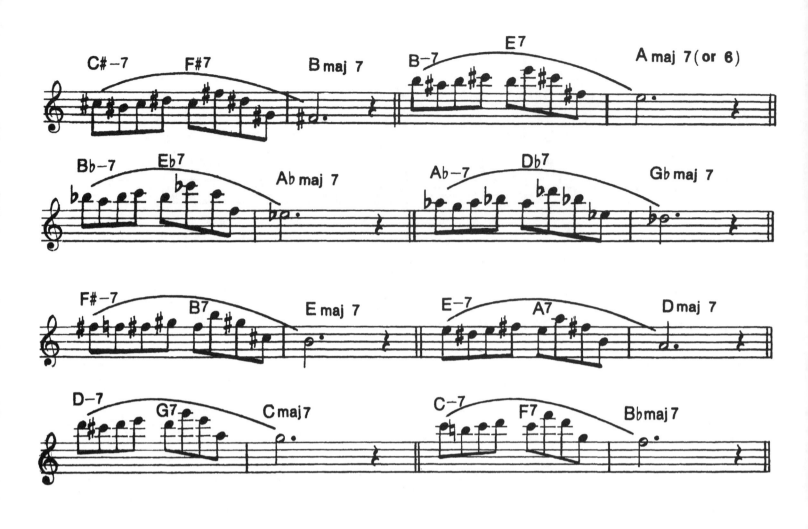

Four Bar Phrases

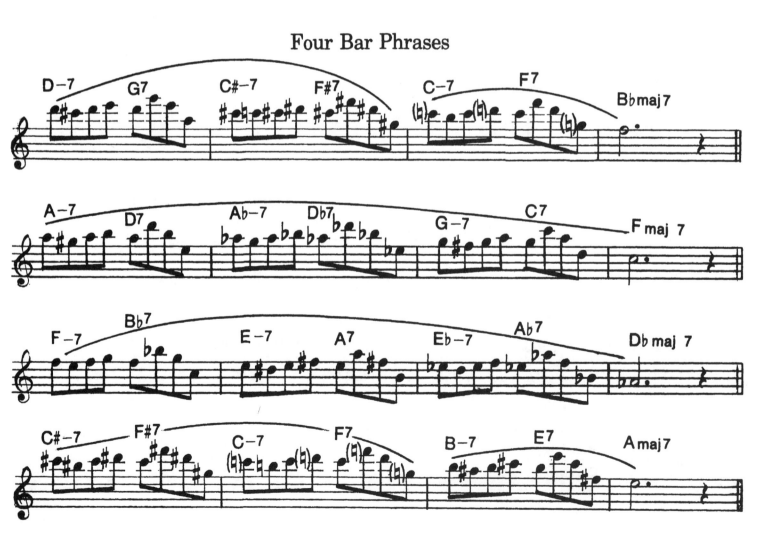

Eight Bar Phrases

Sixteen Bar Phrases

Chapter IV

The Lydian Mode

The Lydian mode is a scale beginning and ending on the fourth degree of the major scale. "F" Lydian would be like a "C" scale beginning and ending on "F."

The Lydian mode is most commonly used in improvisation as the scale relating directly to the IV7 or IV6 chords.

The IV chord in a major key occurs naturally as a major seventh chord. In the key of "C," the IV maj7 chord would be F maj7.

IMPORTANT: While most writers today indicate when the Lydian mode is to be used, usually in this manner; F maj7 or (Lyd), there is sometimes some confusion in certain cases whether to use the Lydian or Ionian mode when a major 7th or 6th chord is given. Note the following example:

| D-7   G7 | C maj 7 | F maj 7 ‖

In this example progression, the key at the moment is "C," and although the C and F chords are both major 7th chords, the C chord is the I chord while the F chord is the IV chord. In cases such as these, try to think in terms of the *function* of the chord as described by the Roman Numerals, such as:

| II-7   V7 | I maj 7 | IV maj 7 ‖

It then becomes quite simple to understand exactly which chord scale or mode to use.

F maj 7 (IV maj 7-Lydian)   *not* F maj 7 (I maj 7-Ionian)

28

29

Exercises through all the keys in Lydian Mode.

Further Examples in the use of the Lydian Mode

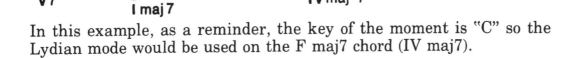

In this example, as a reminder, the key of the moment is "C" so the Lydian mode would be used on the F maj7 chord (IV maj7).

Use F Lydian for F maj 7   *not* F Ionian for F maj 7

As I said earlier in this chapter, most composers now indicate when the Lydian Mode is to be used if there would be any confusion or question involved. In this example, the Lydian Mode is indicated simply because that is the general sound of the tune, and to eliminate any question.

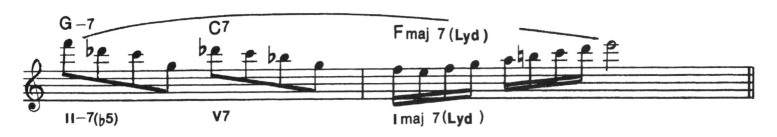

Chapter V

The Lydian Flat Seven

This scale is the first in this book that is not a 'pure' mode. The Lydian flat seven scale is what I call an 'altered modal scale,' in that it is simply the Lydian mode with one note altered; the seventh degree of the scale is lowered (flatted) one half-step.

The Lydian flat seven scale is most commonly used in improvisation as the scale relating directly to the sub V7 (♭II7) chord (i.e. the substitute chord for the V7).

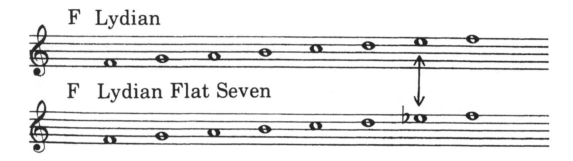

The sub V7 (♭II7) chord is built on the lowered 2nd degree of the major scale. Sub V7 in the key of E would be F7.

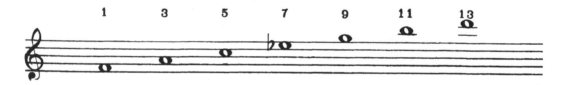

Like the V7 chord, the sub V7 is also a dominant seventh chord and is used in place of the V7 to add color and variety to the normal V7 — I cadence. As seen in the progression below, the V7(G7) is replaced by the sub V7 (D♭7).

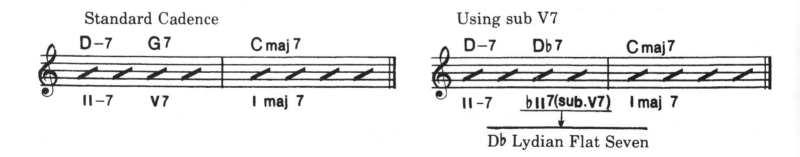

32

34

Earlier in this book you played the chord pattern: II-7 V7 I. The patterns written below are quite similar in function with the exception that instead of using the V7 chord, you will be playing the sub of V7 (which involves using the Lydian flat 7 scale).

Note the connection of the chord scales

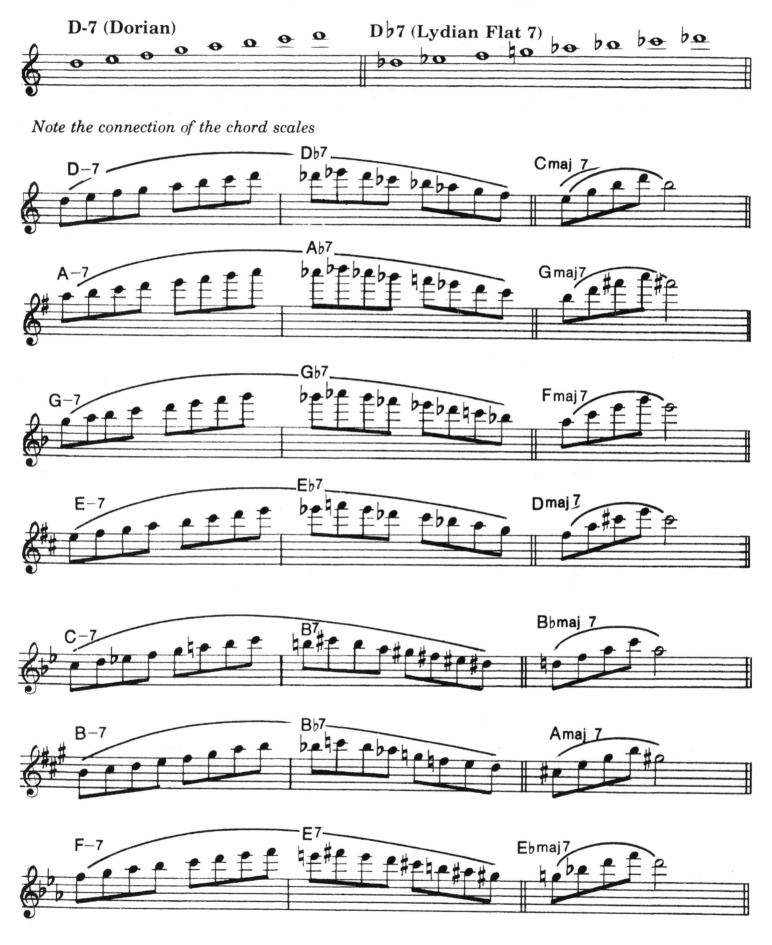

36

Note the connection of the chords

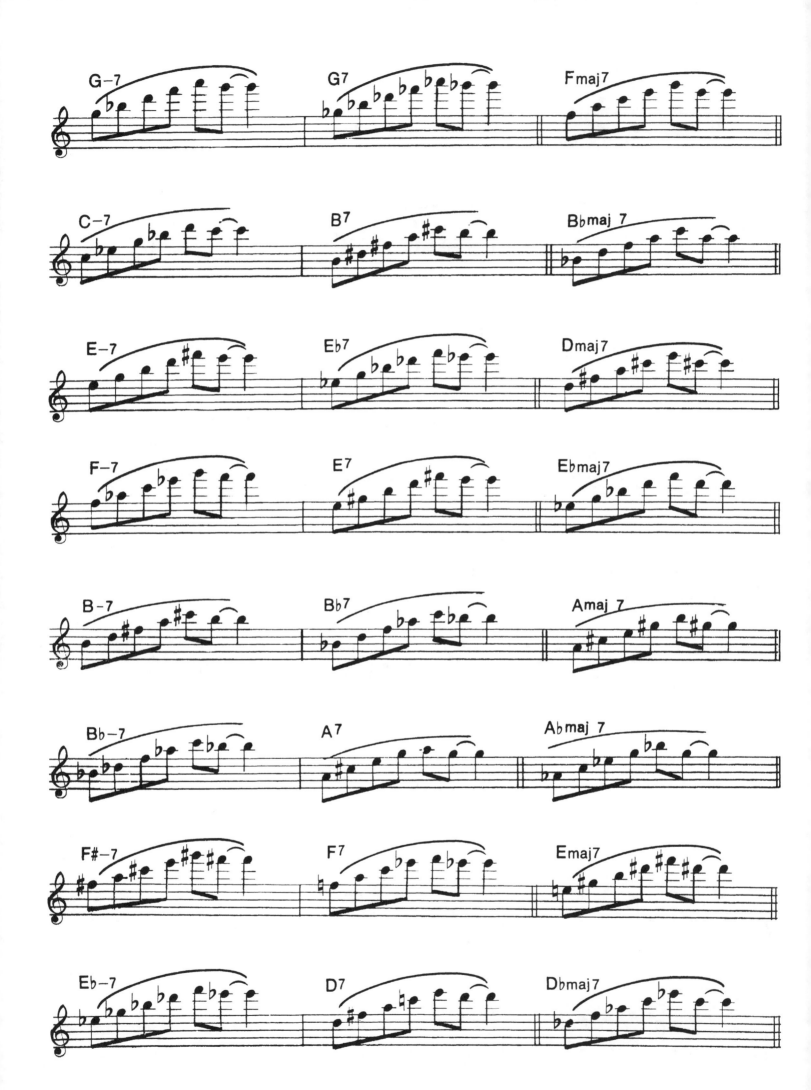

39

Here are some four bar chord progressions which involve the use of the Lydian flat 7 scale. Note how the notes written for each chord change move smoothly through the progression.

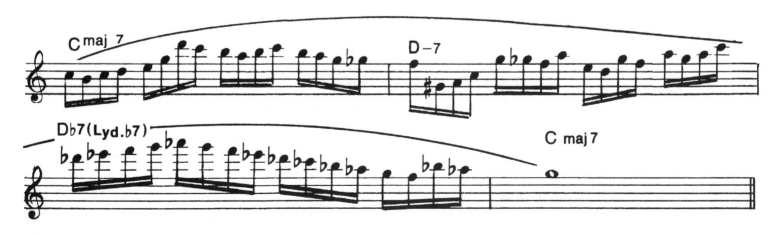

40

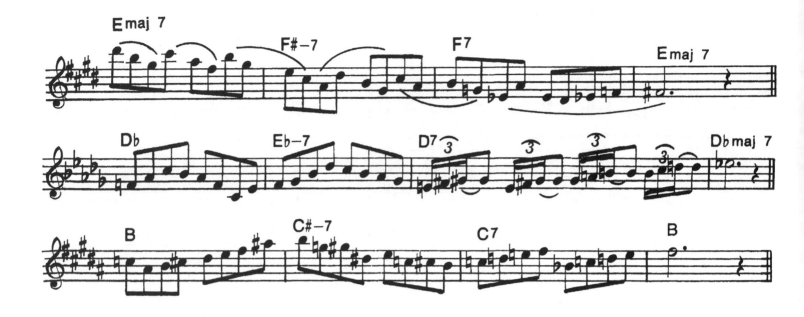

Throughout this section we have used the Lydian flat 7 as a substitute for the V7 chord, but the scale is also used in some other ways. The first, as in the example below, occurs when a II7 (note that this is not diatonic to the key) precedes the II-7 V7 (which are diatonic to the key).

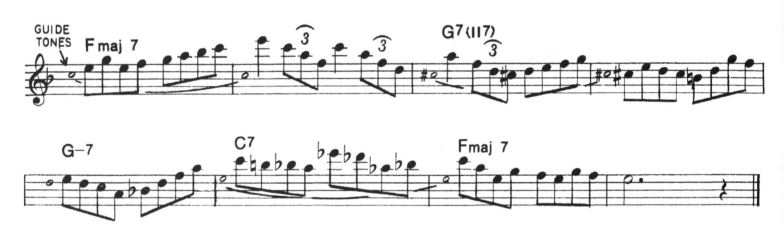

Another use occurs when a modal type cadence ♭VII7-I, rather than the normal V7 (or ♭II7)-I is used, as seen below.

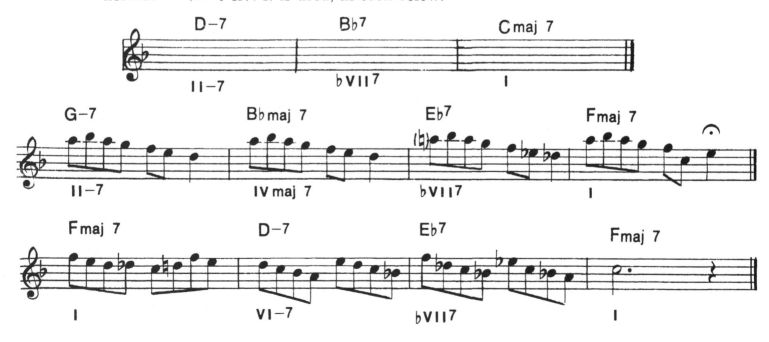

The Lydian flat 7 can also be used to play on the sub of V7 in minor keys as well.

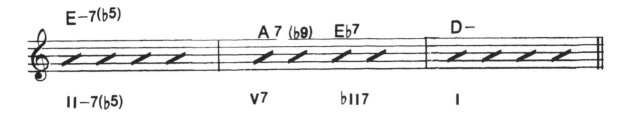

Here is a brief mention of a chord change that is being used more and more in modern music. It is called the "sus 4" chord and will be used in the next few pages. This change is usually written as G(sus 4) Or G7(sus) and the sound is very easy to achieve simply by omitting the 3rd as a chord tone (the 3rd however is OK as a passing tone).

G7(sus) is the same as D-7 with G in the bass, D-7/G bass or D Dorian with G in the bass, D Dorian/G bass. Using this way of thinking, you automatically get the right sound and will not use the 3rd as a chord tone.

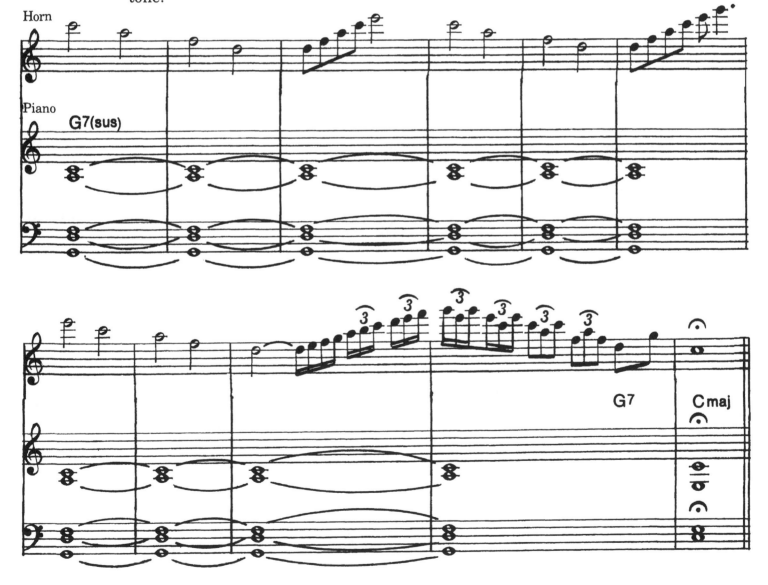

43

Chapter VI

The Diminished Chord and
The Symmetric Diminished Scale

In this chapter, I am going to introduce the chord before the scale. The reason for this is that we will construct the first diminished scale from the notes of the diminished seventh chord.

The diminished seventh chords are very easy to learn because the sound is so unique and moreover, of all the possible ways to indicate the various diminished chords, there are only THREE to remember!

The first is C°7, which includes Eb°7, F#°7 (Gb°7), and A°7.

In these examples you will note that I have simplified some of the chords by using enharmonic spellings where it is practical.

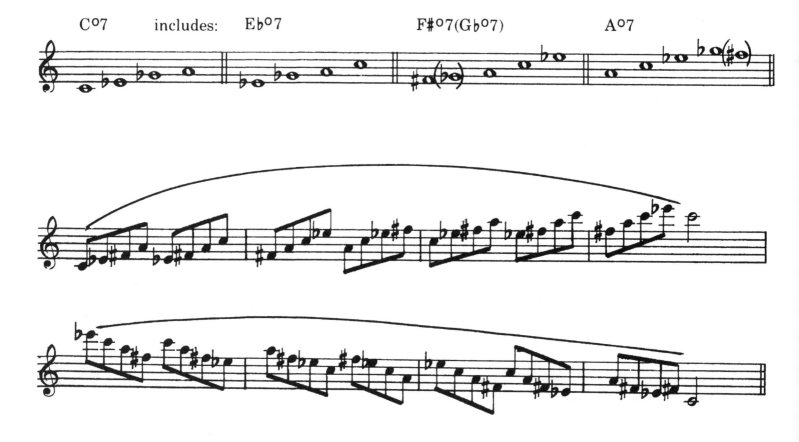

Note: *The following examples also include enharmonic spellings, not only within the chord but each chord shown also includes other enharmonically spelled chords (i.e., the G#7 chord is also the Ab7 chord).*

Now that you are familiar with the diminished chords, its time for a brief introduction to the diminished scales which will be used to play on the diminished chords.

The first diminished scale I'll mention is one that can be used for playing on any diminished chord change. This scale is called the SYMMETRIC DIMINISHED SCALE and is constructed in the same manner for each of the diminished chords.

You begin with any diminished 7th chord, such as C°7

simply by inserting a note a full step above each note in the chord, you have a diminished scale.

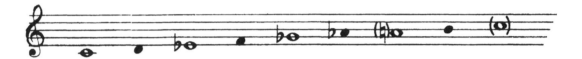

This symmetric diminished scale gets its name from the fact that it is constructed in an absolutely regular or symmetrical manner. Beginning on any note of the chord, the first interval in the scale is a whole step, followed by a half step, followed by a whole step, and so on, so that when the scale is completed it is symmetrical.

whole step ½ step whole step ½ step   whole   ½   whole   ½   etc.

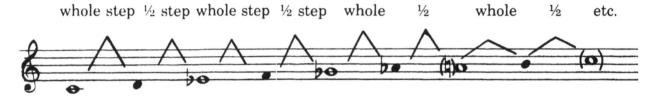

It is interesting to note that, just as with the diminished 7th chords, there are really only three scales to remember. All the possible diminished chord changes can be played with these *three* scales.

46

The C symmetric diminished scale.

Exercises

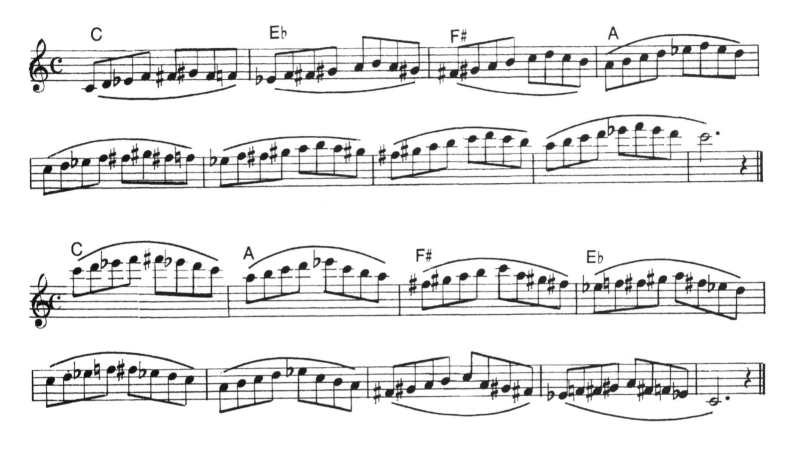

The C♯ symmetric diminished scale

Exercises

The D symmetric diminished scale.

Exercises

Chapter VII

The Sharp I Diminished Scale

The second type of diminished scale, unlike the Symmetric Diminished Scale, is designed for use on a specific scale tone or chord change and also has a specific function.

This scale is called the SHARP I DIMINISHED SCALE and is used when the chord change indicates a sharp I diminished chord($\#I°7$). To eliminate a lot of rules, this scale is constructed from a scale we already know, the Mixolydian. To get a sharp I diminished scale just sharp (raise) the bottom note of the appropriate Mixolydian scale and also add it to the top, giving you a 9 note scale.

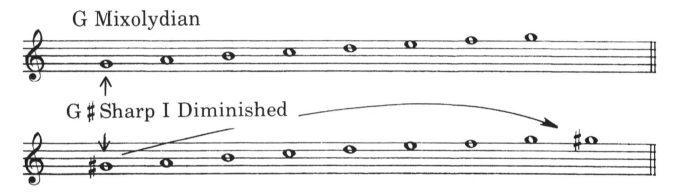

In the last example, the scale was built on G#. In the key of G, the sharp I diminished chord would be G#°7.

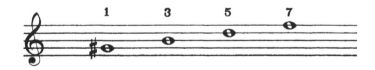

The sharp I diminished chord is probably used most often as a linking chord between the I and II-7 as shown in the following example.

G	G#°7	A−7
I	#I°7	II-7

49

Here are some exercises to help you get the feel of this scale.

Here is a REMINDER of the construction of this scale.

C Mixolydian

9 note diminished scale

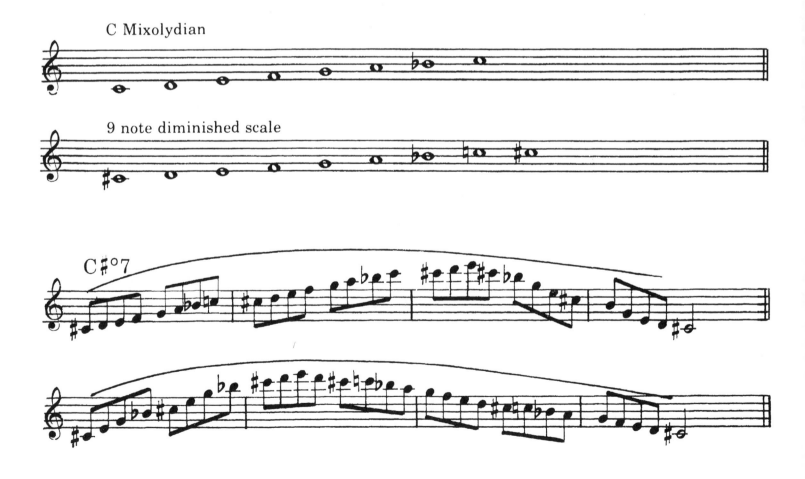

51

Exercises

54

Here are some chord patterns, in all keys, which include the SHARP ONE DIMINISHED chord change and will give you the opportunity to put the ♯I°scale into use. Because these progressions also include the other chord changes we have been studying, you should be able to see and hear more clearly how they all fit together to form a musical phase.

It would be a good idea, after you get the notes under your fingers, to get a piano or guitar player to play the changes while you play the **pattern**. This will help you in two ways. First, it will let you hear exactly the **chord** you are playing on and second, it will help you develop a feeling for time (steady, regular meter) and working with a rhythm section.

Here are the chord changes on which you will be playing.

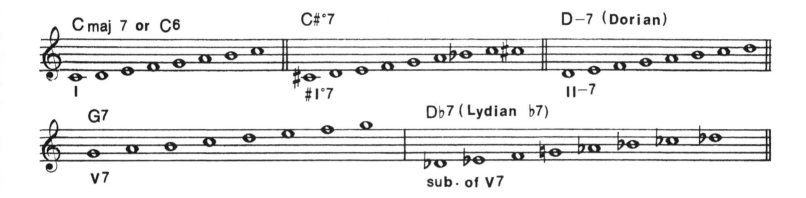

You will notice that I have included both the V7 and the sub. of V7 in this example. There are two examples given in each key in the following patterns. The first uses the V7 and the second, the sub. of V7. Here are the patterns exactly as they are used.

(A)   I - ♯I°7 - II-7 - V7 - I
(B)   I - ♯I°7 - II-7 - sub. of V7 - I

Practice these progressions very slowly at first for control, to help in training the ear and for the smooth connecting of the scales and chords.

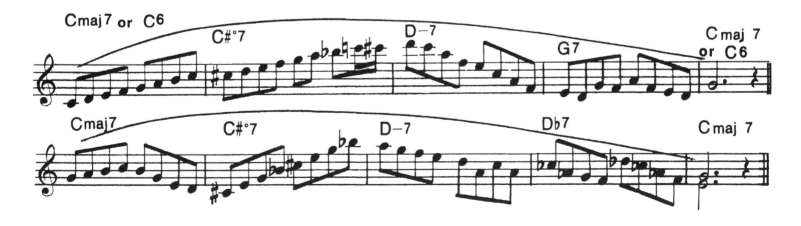

Chapter VIII

The Phrygian Mode

The Phrygian mode has a very unique Eastern-type quality and, perhaps because of this, has not been used to any great extent in modal playing and writing. The scale is used, however, quite extensively in normal chord change situations. The Phrygian mode is a scale beginning and ending on the third degree of the major scale. "E" Phrygian would be like a "C" major scale beginning and ending on "E.".

The Phrygian mode is most commonly applied in improvisation as the scale relating directly to the III-7 chord.

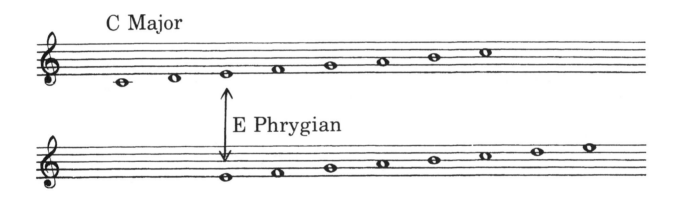

The III-7 chord in a major key occurs naturally as a minor seventh chord. In the key of C, the III-7 chord would be E-7.

A common chord progression using the III-7 change is:

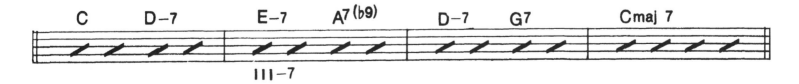

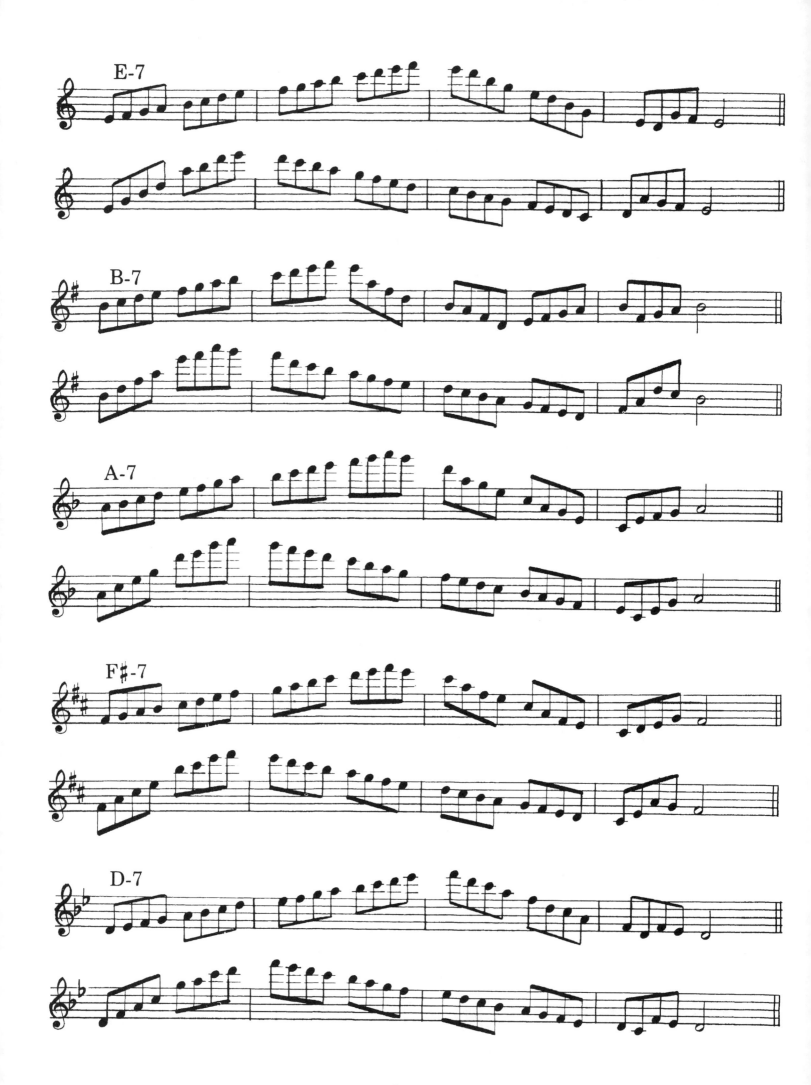

Here are two exercises, the first progressing chromatically and the second through the cycle of fifths, which take a characteristic figure through all the keys.

63

Chapter IX

The Aeolian Mode

The following three chapters will deal with a sound that in traditional western harmony is known as minor. The reason for this is that they all begin and end on the sixth degree of the major diatonic scale. However, you must remember that in modern music, particularly jazz, more and more is being written that stresses a particular quality of sound, individual and unique to each of the modes and altered scales presented here and these modes and scales are not necessarily major or minor as these terms have traditionally been applied.

The first, the Aeolian mode, also known as the natural minor scale, begins and ends on the sixth degree of the major scale. "A" Aeolian would be like a "C" major scale beginning and ending on "A."

The Aeolian mode is most commonly applied in improvisation as the scale relating directly to the VI-7 chord.

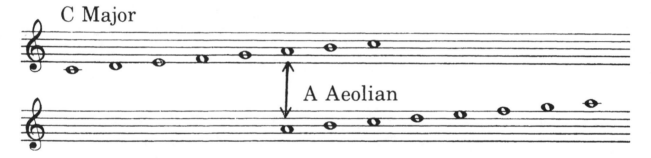

The VI-7 chord in a major key occurs naturally as a minor seventh chord. In the key of C, the VI-7 chord would be A-7.

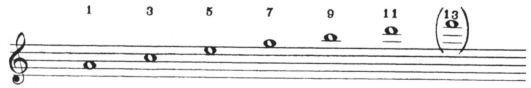

A common chord progression using the VI-7 change is:

You will also see this scale in a tune that is purely modal. The writer will indicate this by writing Aeolian, usually in conjunction with changes or tonality indicated of some type, as seen in this example.

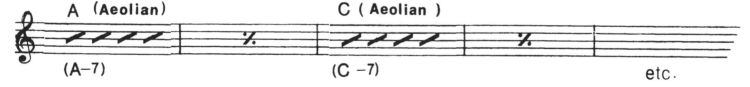

64

Exercises

66

Chapter X

The Jazz Melodic Minor Scale

The jazz melodic minor scale is used when playing on a minor sixth chord change, such as A-6 and looks like this.

A Jazz Melodic Minor

A-6

Notice that the scale is played both UP and Down with the raised 6th and 7th. This differs from the traditional melodic minor, shown below, that has the raised 6th and 7th only when ascending.

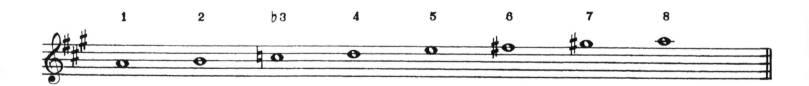

Another way to think of this scale would be: a major scale with flatted (lowered) 3rd gives you the jazz melodic minor scale.

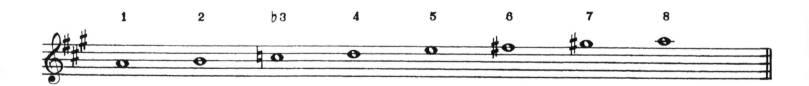

Exercises

A-6

E-6

D-6

B-6

71

Exercises

Minor sixth chords with the 9th and 11th added

Chapter XI

The Harmonic Minor Scale

The next minor scale is the HARMONIC MINOR scale. The traditional
and jazz versions of this scale are exactly the same, simply a natural
minor scale with the seventh raised. This scale may be used with the
minor (+7) chord, a minor triad with a raised seventh, ex: A-(+7).

A Harmonic Minor   A-(+7)

Exercises

73

74

75

Harmonic Minor Chord with +7, 9, 11.

In a minor key, the V7 chord often has a flatted 9th (♭9) added to the chord, so that it might be written V7(♭9) or as in the key of A minor, E7(♭9) The flat 9 is used because it makes the need for V7 to resolve even stronger and, in minor, the 9 is naturally lowered (flatted).

A-(+7)

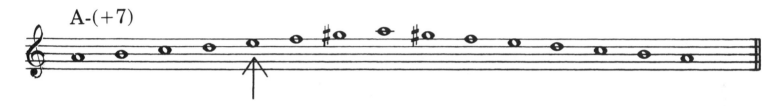

The scale we will use to play on the V7(♭9) chord is the one we have just been using, the harmonic minor scale. There will be just one difference, however, as you can see below. Instead of beginning on the first degree of the scale, we begin on the fifth.

E7(♭9)   E7(♭9)

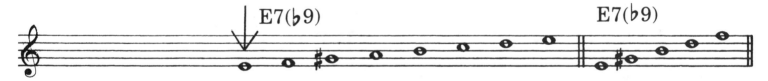

Exercises

A-(+7)

E7(♭9)

E7(♭9)

77

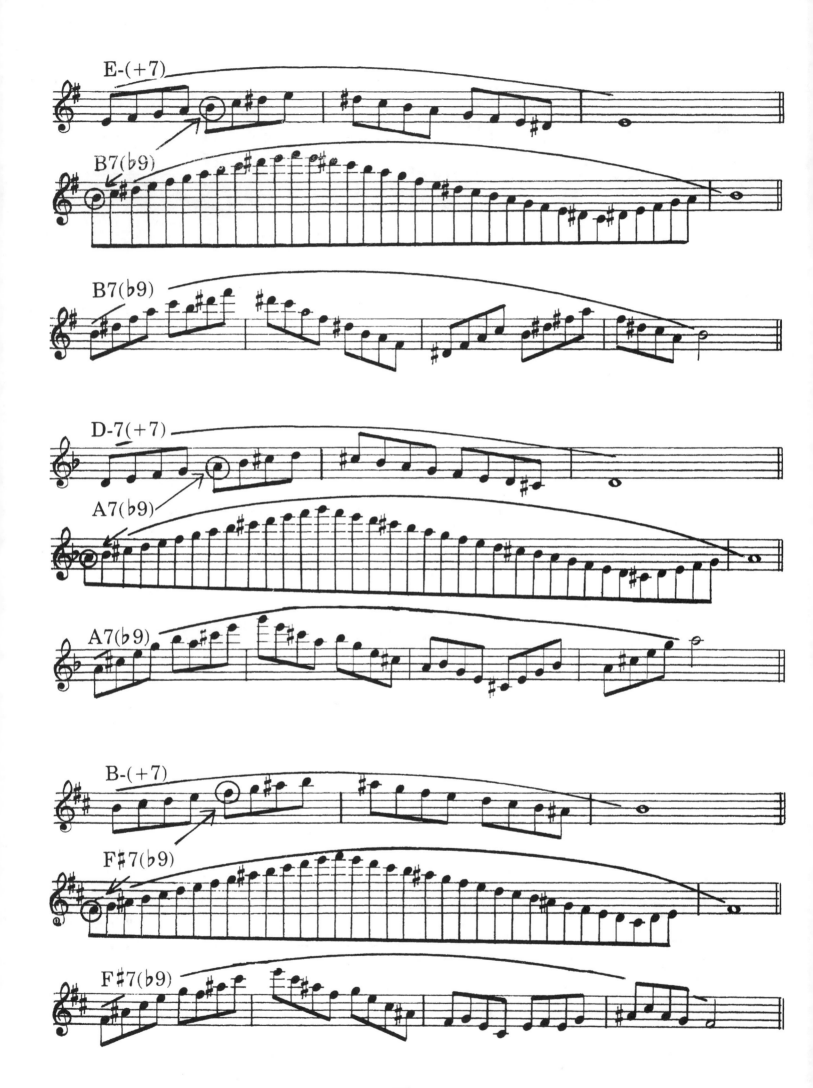

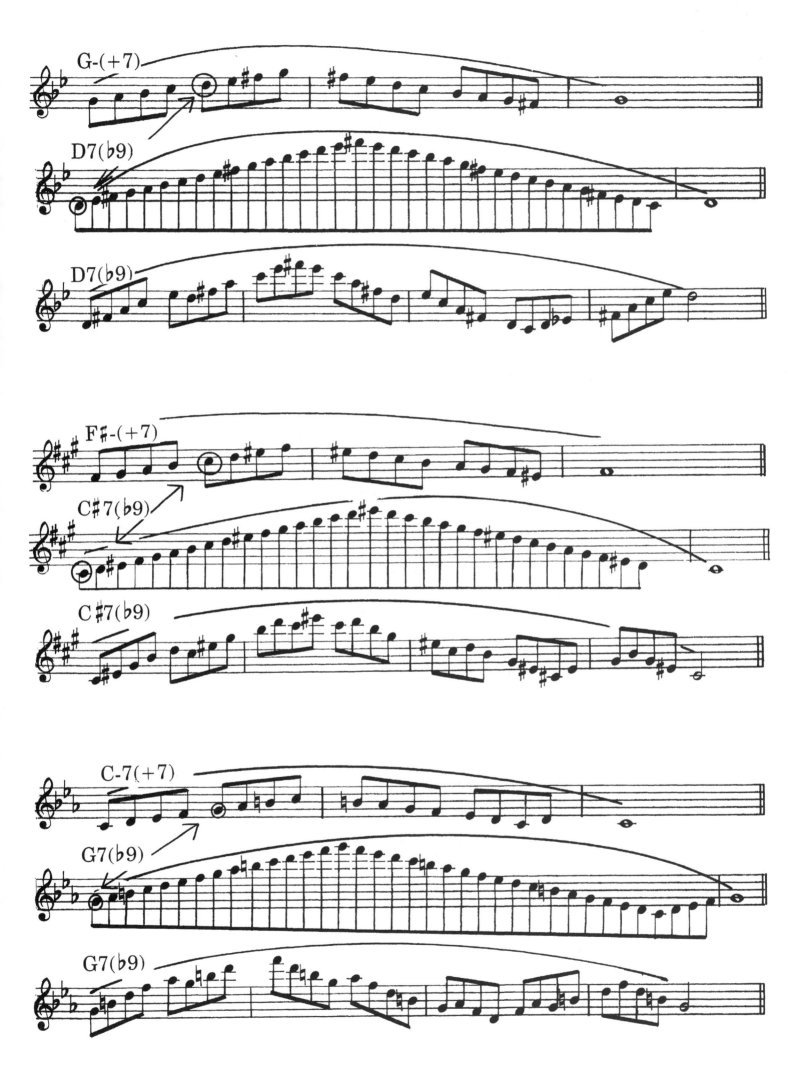

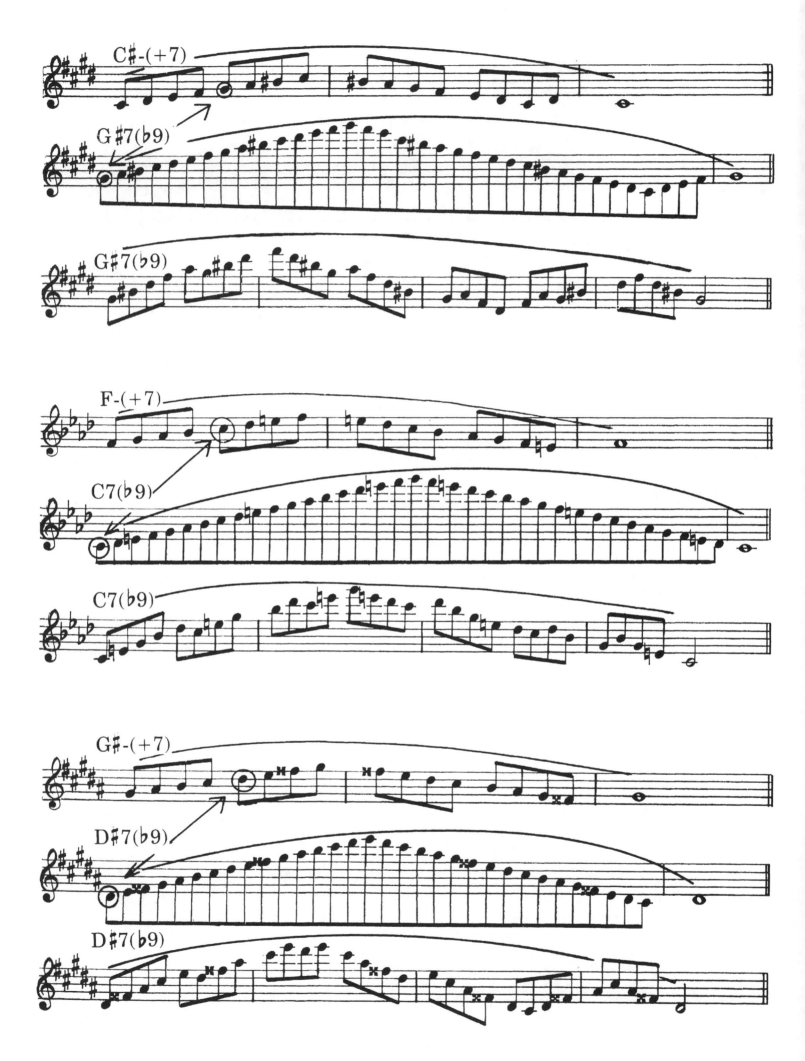

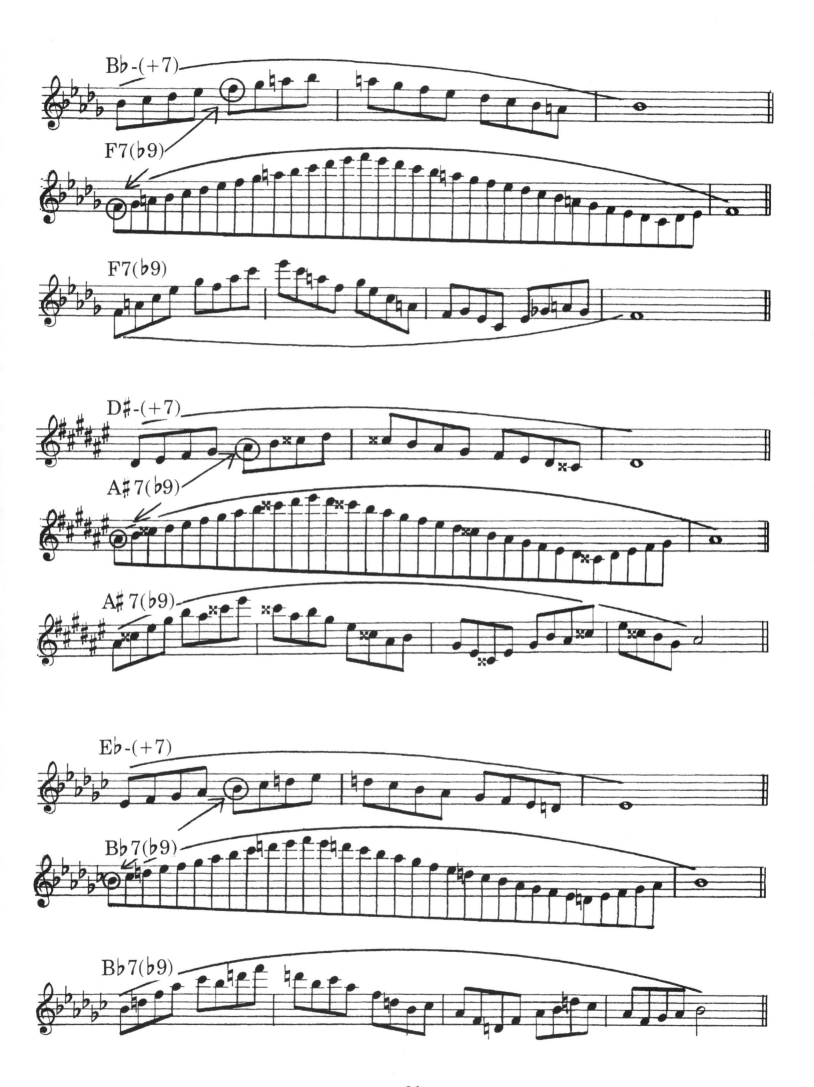

Chapter XII

The Locrian Mode

The introduction of the Locrian mode completes all of the modal scales. The Locrian mode is a scale beginning and ending on the 7th degree of the major scale. "B" Locrian would be like a "C" scale beginning and ending on "B".

The Locrian mode is most often used in improvisation in the minor tonality as the scale relating directly to the II chord of the minor key (the VII chord in a major key).

C Major

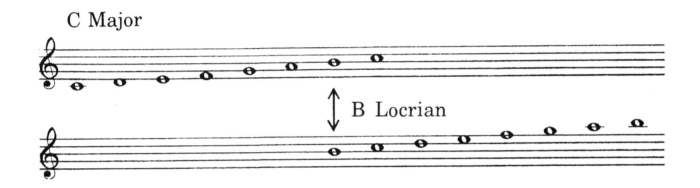

The II chord in a minor key (and the VII in a major key) occurs naturally as a minor 7th flat 5 chord (half diminished in traditional terminology). In the key of A minor, the II chord would be B-7(♭5).

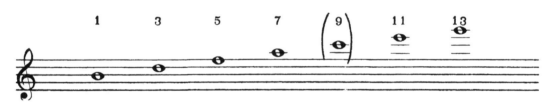

Exercises

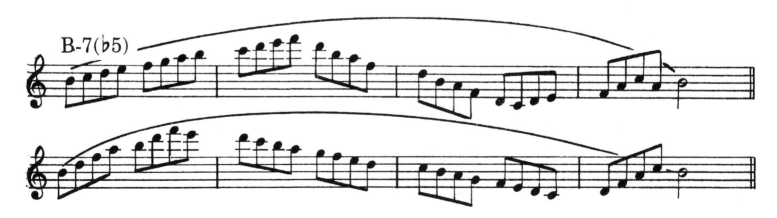

83

84

Chapter XIII

Exercises applying material
from the last four chapters

Now it's time to apply these minor scales and modes to minor tonality
chord changes. The first pattern is the II to V.

NOTE: *All of the exercises using the II minor 7(♭5) and the V7(♭9) can be played with ease if you know the major scales and the harmonic minor scales. You should review your scales as a warm-up exercise daily. One day warm up with major scales, the next day, minor.*

This next set of exercises are 4 bar phrases using the chord pattern:

II-7(♭5) V7(♭9) I-

Each phrase is written in four different keys. Play them slowly at first to get the notes under your fingers and to get used to the sound of the phrase. I'd like to mention once again to try to get together with a piano or guitar player, and let them play the changes while you play the phrases.

The following four bar phrases are given in only one key. After playing each pattern in the key given, play the same pattern in another key of your choice, by ear.

Chapter XIV

The Turn Back

This common progression is standard in popular music and jazz and is most commonly used in the first ending or the last two bars of a tune. It is a device used to keep the tune from ending, to "turn back" to the beginning, either where you would naturally turn back (as in a first ending) but where there is limited chord or harmonic action, or at the end of a song, to turn it back to the top to play another chorus.

Although turn backs can take many forms, we will deal with some of the standard patterns used by good jazz players in sessions all over the world.

The changes are: I - V7 of II - II-7 - V7

or as a substitute   I -#I°- II-7 - bII7

Here is a sample of a 'lead sheet' or sheet music 1st ending.

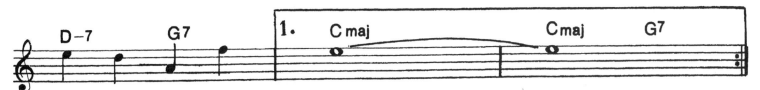

Here is the same melody with a turn back added.

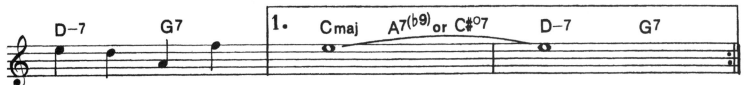

This example shows how the turn back would fit in at the end of a tune, to keep it going.

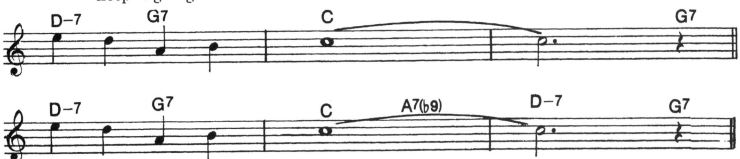

NOTE: *The C in the melody when played with the A7(b9) chord becomes a +9 and is good to use with the b9. The C in the melody when played with the G7 chord becomes a sus. 4, which I have earlier explained.*

Here are the two turn back patterns. The first is the original and the second is using substitute chords

(A)	C	A7(♭9)	D-7	G7
(B)	C	C♯°7	D-7	D♭7

Any of these chords can be substituted for any other at any time. The C♯°7 can be played against the A7(♭9) and the D♭7 (Lyd. flat 7) can be played against the G7.

The following exercises are two turn back phrases written in all the keys. Play them slowly at first to help develop your ear.

96

Here are two more turn back phrases written in all the keys.

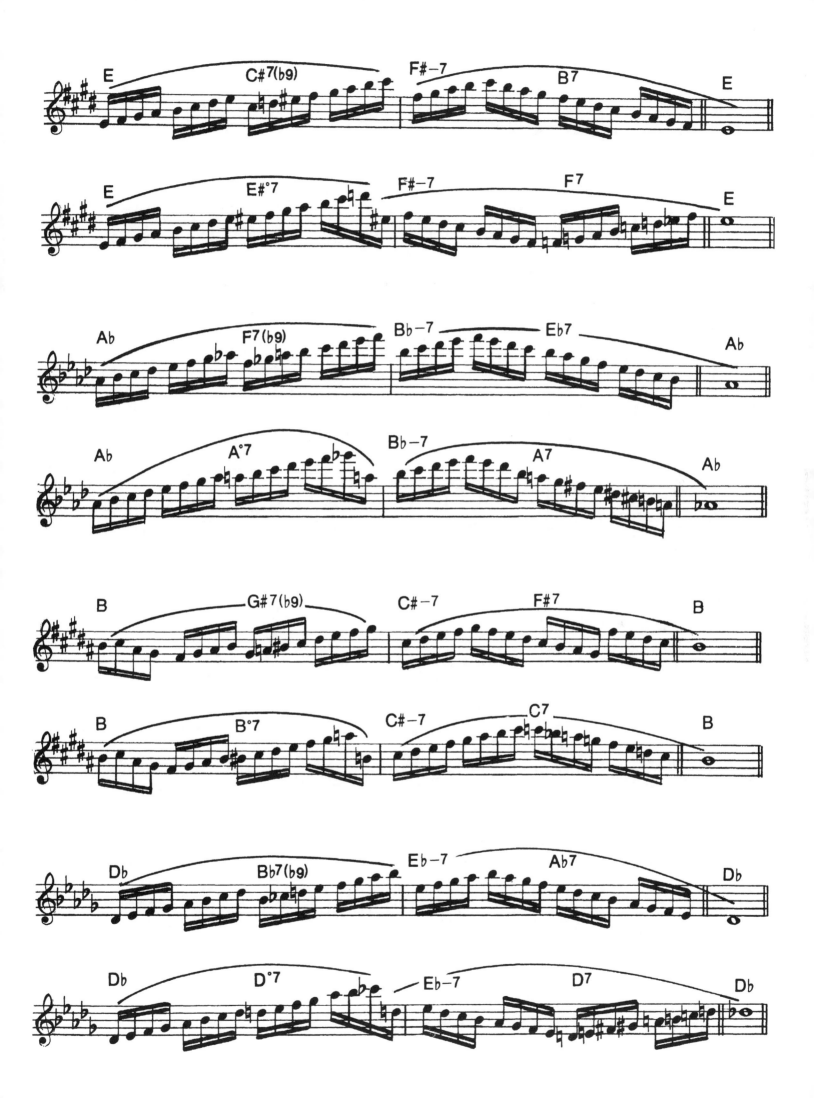

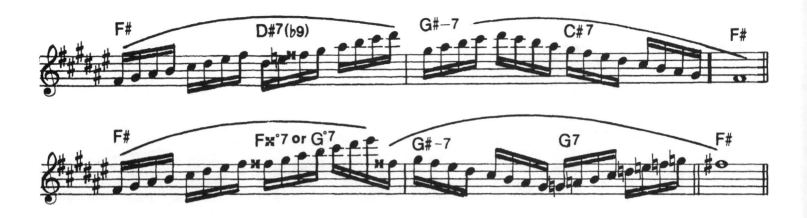

Play these patterns first as they are written, then transpose them by ear to another key of your choice.

Chapter XV

Augmented Chords and
The Whole Tone Scale

The augmented chord, indicated by a +, as in C+, is quite easy to learn and relates harmonically to the whole tone scale. There are only four versions of the augmented chord to learn and remember and, in the following examples, I will simplify even further by including enharmonic spellings where practical.

An augmented chord is a major triad with the 5th raised.

C+   (C Aug)   includes: E+   and G♯ +

To simplify these chords, just remember these three notes: C, E and G♯ When playing it isn't necessary to remember the theoretical structure of the chord.

D+ (D Aug.)   includes F♯+   and A♯+   (B♭+)

To simplify remember: D ,   F♯ and B♭.

D+

105

By combining these two augmented chords (C and D) you get a Whole Tone scale, the first two.

C+   D+   Combined to form a Whole Tone Scale

Play this slowly to get used to the sound.

C whole tone scale

D whole tone scale

E whole tone scale

F♯ whole tone scale

G# whole tone scale

Bb whole tone scale

Notice that the notes included in each of the preceding scales are the same.

NOTE: *When you see any of these changes (or their enharmonic equivalents): C+, D+, E+, F♯+, G♯+ and B♭+, you can use any of the scales interchangeably because they are all essentially the same.*

Here are some patterns using this whole tone scale

The next pair of augmented chords begins with E♭+.

Simplified: remember E♭, G and B

The last augmented chord is F+

Simplified: remember F, A and C♯

109

Combining the E♭ + and F+ will give you the other whole tone scale.
(remember there are only two)

Here are some patterns using this whole tone scale

Here are some phrases using the augmented chords and whole tone scales in the chord changes.

Chapter XVI

This section includes a few tunes and changes to give you a better idea of exactly how the techniques presented in this book can be applied to actual session type playing. Again I mention that to get the most out of this section, get together with a piano or guitar player, or, if possible, a whole rhythm section. Any of the tunes and solos in this section can be expanded to any length simply be repeating the tune or by using the turn-back. But most importantly play, play, PLAY!!

My Two

My Two con't.

Solo

repeat melody

Either Way

(Mixolydian)

Rock or Jazz

Melody

Solo

repeat melody

116

Mr. T.

(Lydian)

This ballad utilizes many of the techniques presented in this book. Note that in the written improvisation section, the original melody was, in spots, repeated exactly as first presented. This is a good idea when playing ballads because it adds continuity and structure to the solo. Always try to learn the original melody well before attempting to improvise on it.

Sweet Con

Sweet Con con't.

Solo

Solo on Blues Changes

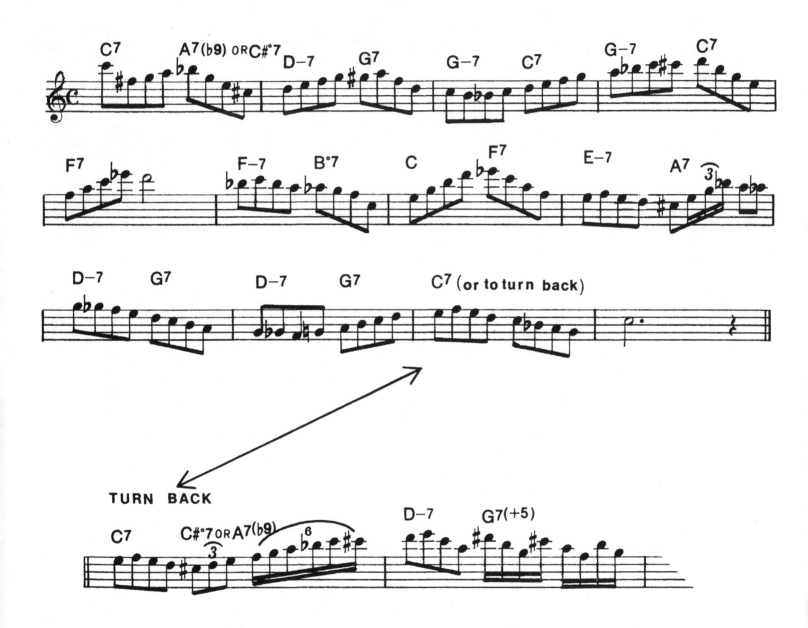